Secrets of Making Frozen Desserts At Home

150 Tested Recipes

HOW TO FREEZE ICE CREAM AT HOME

Freezing

1—Scald the freezer can to be sure it is clean and sweet.

2—Prepare the mixture to be frozen, as described in the recipes in this book. Place the mixture in the freezer can.

3—Assemble the freezer ready for freezing.

Packing

4—Chip the ice in small pieces and mix with coarse ice cream salt in the proportion of 3 to 6 parts of ice to one of salt. The 3 to 1 mixture may be used if quicker freezing is desired, but a larger swell is obtained by using the 6 to 1 mixture.

5—Pack ice and salt around the freezer can up to the top, turn the crank a few times to set the ice and salt, then add more ice and salt until the top of the can is covered.

6—Start turning the crank, slowly at first; as the mixture begins to stiffen, turn rapidly to secure the desired beating. The special design of the dasher makes it possible to blend and whip the cream to a delightful mellowness.

7—If the directions have been followed, from three to five minutes should be sufficient to freeze the cream enough to serve at once. When frozen, be sure that the waste hole is not plugged up; pour off some of the brine until the level of brine is well below the cover of the can. Remove the top of the freezer and take off the can cover. Insert a cork in the can cover to stop up the hole in the top. Remove the dasher and scrape the ice cream into the can. Place cover on the can and add more ice and salt to the level of the cover. It is a good idea to cover the freezer with a thick pad of newspapers or a heavy cloth to keep the air from the ice.

8—Allow the ice cream to "set" in this freezing mixture until time for serving.

Molding the Cream

9—When time comes for serving, if desired, the cream may be turned out in a solid form by removing the can and wrapping it in a cloth wrung out of hot water. By hitting the can, the ice cream will slip out on to a platter or serving dish. Be sure that the cream is tampt down thoroughly before it is allowed to "set" if you wish the cream to be served in cylinder form.

10—Many hostesses like to serve their ice cream in a mold. In this case, when the mixture is frozen, place it in the mold and pack it down well so that it will come out in a perfect shape. If two or three varieties of cream are used, smooth off each layer before adding the next one, smooth cream on top and cover with a piece of greased and waxed paper (greased side up) cut larger than the mold.

Place mold in the top of packed ice and salt so that there is a layer of salt and ice under the mold, with the top completely buried. Let it freeze for from two to three hours.

To remove, wipe the mold with a cloth. Remove the cover and allow the mold to stand for several minutes in a warm place.

WAYS OF SERVING FROZEN DESSERTS

Candied rose leaves, violets, and other flowers may be found in shops making a specialty of them and are decorative to any cream or ice when placed over the top or as a border around the edge of dish. Slices of angel cake or sponge cake may be placed in ice cream dishes, a little fruit syrup poured over each slice, then a half of a peach or slice of pineapple. Fill up the dish with vanilla ice cream with a tablespoonful of whipped cream on top; decorate with candied fruit.

Place ice cream on small glass plates, pour over one tablespoon of crushed sweetened strawberries or other fruits. Top with sweetened whipped cream, or with any desired prepared sauce. See recipes for sauces.

To make Croquettes: Take ice cream from freezer with a scoop, roll in blanched almonds which have been chopped fine and browned in the oven. Serve in glass plates surrounded with following sauce: Beat up whites of three eggs until stiff, add 1 cup double cream and beat until stiff again, add one-half cup of sugar, one teaspoon orange extract, and one-half cup chopped preserved cherries.

To make Sandwiches: Cut cake into slices, cut slices of ice cream and put between slices of cake. Decorate with powdered macaroons.

Scoop out the pulp of well-flavored cantaloupes and half fill tall lemonade glasses with melon seasoned with a little lemon juice and powdered sugar and dash of cinnamon. Fill up glasses with vanilla ice cream. Decorate with candied lemon or orange peel. To serve Bisque: Arrange lady fingers or oblong sweet wafers in box shape on ice cream plate and tie in place with narrow ribbon. Fill with bisque. Decorate with candied flowers.

Remove peeling from bananas and split lengthwise. Sprinkle with powdered sugar and lemon juice. Arrange on oblong ice cream dishes;

place ice cream on bananas, pour over crushed berries, top with sweetened whipped cream. Decorate with maraschino cherries.

ICE CREAMS

Apple Mint Ice Cream
(Makes 2 quarts)

    2 oz. bitter chocolate
    1½ cups sweet milk
    1 egg white
    ¾ cup apple jelly
    1 cup whipping cream
    3 drops oil peppermint flavoring

Cut chocolate into small pieces. Add to milk, and heat until chocolate is melted, beating occasionally to blend the chocolate with the milk. Cool. Whip egg white and jelly together until stiff. Add to chocolate milk, mixing thoroughly. Add mint flavoring and fold in whipped cream. Stir mixture thoroughly and chill. Freeze.

Banana Ice Cream
(Makes 2 quarts)

    1 cup banana pulp
    1½ cups confectioners' sugar
    2 cups heavy cream
    ⅛ tsp. nutmeg
    1 tbs. powdered gelatine
    2 eggs
    1½ cups milk
    1 tbs. lemon juice
    ⅛ tsp. salt
    2 tbs. cold water

Beat eggs and sugar until light; add salt, nutmeg, milk, and gelatine which has been softened in the cold water and dissolved over a pan of hot water. Crush bananas with a silver fork to a fine pulp, stir in lemon juice, and add to mixture. Whip cream and add. Freeze.

Caramel Ice Cream
(Makes 2 quarts)

¼ cup sugar
½ cup water
2 egg yolks
½ cup sugar
¼ cup flour
1½ cups milk
½ tsp. vanilla
½ tsp. maplene flavoring
1 cup whipping cream

Heat ¼ cup sugar until it is melted. Cook 2 minutes, then add ½ cup water and stir until sugar is dissolved. Cook until syrup spins a thread. Pour gradually over egg yolks that have been beaten until light lemon colored, beating constantly. Blend ½ cup sugar and flour, add milk, and cook until thickened, stirring thoroughly and frequently. Add egg yolk mixture and cook several minutes longer. Cool. Stir in flavorings and fold in whipped cream. Freeze.

Chocolate Ice Cream
(Makes 2 quarts)

1½ cups milk
1½ cups confectioners' sugar
6 tbs. grated chocolate
2½ cups heavy cream
2 eggs
2 tbs. cold water
1 tbs. vanilla extract

Beat eggs and sugar until light. Stir the cold water into chocolate and dissolve over hot water, then add to eggs and sugar. Stir in milk—strain through fine sieve. Flavor with vanilla, add salt to cream, and whip until stiff. Fold this into mixture. Freeze.

Chocolate Ice Cream
(Makes 2 quarts)

2½ sqs. chocolate cut into small pieces
¼ tsp. salt
2 cups milk
1 cup sugar
2 eggs
4 drops almond flavoring
1 tbs. vanilla
1 cup whipping cream

Melt the chocolate in a double boiler, add the salt, milk, and sugar, and scald thoroughly. Beat to blend the mixture. Separate the eggs and pour a little of this mixture slowly over the beaten egg yolks. Return all to the double boiler and cook until slightly thickened. Chill, add flavorings, and fold in the egg whites beaten stiff, then the cream whipped. Freeze.

Mrs. O. E. Frisbie, Wyoming.

Coffee Ice Cream
(Makes 2 quarts)

3 cups milk
1½ cups sugar
2 tbs. arrowroot
2 cups cream
6 tbs. ground coffee
2 eggs

Scald the coffee and milk to boiling point; strain through cheesecloth. Beat eggs, sugar, and arrowroot together, stir in milk, and cook in a double boiler until mixture thickens. Remove from fire and when cold add cream whipped stiff. Freeze.

Sour Cream Ice Cream

The cream may be thick sour and used with perfect safety, so that the most fastidious person could not detect it. It is not only a matter of economy but makes a much richer cream than the same amount when sweet.

For chocolate, make a custard of one quart of milk, two eggs, one cup of sugar, and one tablespoon of flour. Melt two squares of chocolate and add to the custard. When cold, flavor with one teaspoon of vanilla. Just before freezing, add one pint of sweet milk, one cup of sugar, and one pint of sour cream and beat until thoroughly mixed. Freeze as usual.

Sour cream may be used with other custards in a similar manner, adding after the custard is cool, beating thoroughly. It is especially delicious with fruits.

Date Ice Cream
(Makes 4 quarts)

1 lb. dates
4 tbs. orange juice
1 qt. cream
1 egg
1 tsp. flour
1 cup sugar
⅛ tsp. salt
2 cups scalded milk

Wash and seed the dates and put through food chopper. Mix with orange juice ½ cup cream and blend by setting mixture in double boiler over the flame. Mix the flour, sugar, and salt, and add to scalded milk. Cook over boiling water for 10 minutes. Pour slowly over the lightly beaten egg and cook over water for 5 minutes, stirring constantly. Cool and add remaining 3½ cups cream, and lastly the date mixture. Freeze.

Ginger-Orange Ice Cream
(Makes 4 quarts)

2 oranges
2 cups hot water
3 cups cold water
1½ tsp. ginger
1¼ cups sugar
Grated rind of 1 lemon
3 egg whites, beaten stiff
2 cups heavy cream, whipped

Peel the oranges, shred the peel, and add 1 cup hot water. Boil for 5 minutes, then drain and discard the water. Add another cup hot water and ginger. Boil again for 5 minutes, drain, and discard the peel. Make a syrup of this water, the sugar, and the grated lemon rind. When the sugar is dissolved, add the orange pulp which has been cut into small pieces and all the fibre and membranes removed. Simmer for 2 or 3 minutes. Remove from the stove, cool, and add the remaining 3 cups cold water and freeze to a mush. Beat the egg whites until stiff, fold in the whipped cream, and stir into the half-frozen fruit mixture. Continue freezing until firm. Allow the ice cream to ripen in the freezer for 3 or 4 hours. Serve in sherbet glasses with lemon-flavored golden sponge cake.

Mrs. G. K. Foot, Montana.

Golden Glow Ice Cream
(Makes 4 quarts)

2 qts. milk
1 tbs. flour
1 qt. can apricots
2 cups sugar
1 cup hot water

2 oranges
1 cup grated pineapple

Boil sugar and water 5 minutes. Add pineapple, apricots, cut fine, with juice, and juice and pulp of oranges. Scald milk, add flour moistened with 2 tbs. milk, and cook 2 minutes. Blend with the fruit mixture, cool, and freeze.

Grape-Nuts Ice Cream
(Makes 4 quarts)

1 qt. whole milk
½ cup dark brown sugar
½ cup sugar
2 eggs
1 tsp. vanilla
⅛ tsp. salt
2 junket tablets dissolved in 1 tbs. cold water
1 cup whipping cream
⅓ cup Grape-Nuts

Heat the milk until lukewarm and add the sugars. Separate the eggs, and add the yolks well beaten, the vanilla, salt, and dissolved junket tablets. Stir thoroughly and chill. Then fold in the egg whites beaten stiff and the cream whipped and combined with the Grape-Nuts. Stir thoroughly to mix all the ingredients. Freeze.

Miss G. B. Dolezal, Iowa.

Lemon Ice Cream
(Makes 2 quarts)

3 eggs
1¼ cups sugar
1 cup cream
1 tbs. vanilla
1 tbs. lemon flavoring

1½ qts. milk

Beat the eggs until light. Add the sugar and continue beating until smooth. Add the cream and the flavorings and mix thoroughly. Add vanilla and freeze. When the desired consistency, remove the paddle and pack the ice cream in salt and ice mixture. 1 qt. of crushed strawberries (sweetened) may be added to the ice cream if desired or the plain ice cream is delicious served with chocolate sauce.

Mrs. D. Morgan, Nebraska.

Marshmallow Ice Cream
(Makes 2 quarts)

40 marshmallows
2 cups milk
1 pt. whipping cream
2 tbs. vanilla

Place the marshmallows and milk over hot water and stir until the marshmallows are melted. Remove from the heat, add the vanilla, and cool. When chilled and beginning to thicken, fold in the cream whipped until thick but not stiff. Freeze. (2 squares of melted chocolate added to the hot mixture makes a pleasing variation.)

Mrs. R. G. McQueary, Colorado.

Nut and Raisin Ice Cream
(Makes 2 quarts)

1 cup raisins
1 cup pecans or walnuts
2 cups milk
1 qt. thin cream
1 tbs. flour
1 cup sugar
1 tbs. vanilla

Pinch of salt

Grind nuts and raisins fine. Cover with some of the milk and stand on low flame until thoroughly mixed. Add sugar, flour, and salt to cream and milk, flavor with vanilla, and put into freezer. When half frozen, add the cooled mixture of nuts, raisins, and milk. Finish freezing.

Prune Ice Cream
(Makes 2 quarts)

1 lb. prunes
Juice 1 lemon
1½ cups sugar
3 cups milk
1 cup cream
½ tsp. salt

Wash prunes, soak overnight, and cook slowly in water to cover until tender. Then add sugar and lemon juice. Allow to simmer 10 minutes. Strain juice. Seed prunes and put pulp and juice through potato ricer. Add to milk, cream, and salt. Cool and freeze.

Peach Ice Cream
(Makes 2 quarts)

1 cup milk
1 cup sugar
2 tbs. flour
2 cups mushed peach pulp
2 tbs. lemon juice
1 cup whipping cream

Combine sugar and flour, add milk, and cook until thick, stirring occasionally. Cool. Add peach pulp and lemon juice. Fold in whipped cream. Freeze.

Strawberry Ice Cream (Cooked)
(Makes 4 quarts)

    1 cup milk
    2 cups crushed berries
    2 cups sugar
    2 cups heavy cream
    3 eggs
    1 tbs. flour or cornstarch
    ⅛ tsp. salt

Scald milk and stir thoroughly and slowly into well-beaten eggs 1 cup of sugar, salt, and flour. Cook in double boiler, stirring constantly until mixture thickens. Remove from fire and when cold fold in cream whipped stiff. When partially frozen, stir in thoroughly the strawberries which have been crushed and pressed through a sieve and sweetened with remaining sugar. Freeze.

Strawberry Ice Cream
(Makes 2 quarts)

    1 cup milk, scalded
    ¾ cup sugar
    2 tbs. flour
    1 qt. strawberries
    1 cup whipping cream

Combine ½ cup sugar and flour. Gradually add scalded milk and cook until thick. Cool. Add strawberries that have been forced through sieve and to which the remaining ¼ cup sugar has been added and dissolved. Fold in whipped cream. Freeze.

Strawberry Ice Cream
(Makes 4 quarts)

    2½ cups milk
    1½ cups confectioners' sugar

3 eggs
1 tbs. powdered gelatine
2½ cups heavy cream
1 tbs. vanilla extract
2 tbs. cold water
⅛ tsp. salt
2 cups crushed sweetened strawberries

Beat eggs and sugar until light, add gelatine which has been softened in the cold water and dissolved over boiling water. Stir in milk, add vanilla, cream, to which salt has been added, whipped until stiff, in an ice-cold bowl. Press strawberries through a sieve, sweeten and stir into mixture. Freeze.

Six Threes Ice Cream
(Makes 4 quarts)

3 cups milk
3 cups cream
3 cups sugar
Juice of 3 lemons
Juice of 3 oranges
3 bananas, mashed

Combine the milk, cream, and sugar and stir until the sugar is dissolved. Place in an ice-cream freezer and freeze until thoroughly chilled and of a mushy consistency. Add the fruit juices and the mashed bananas and continue freezing until firm. Remove the dasher and pack in salt and ice for several hours. This makes about 1 gallon.

Mrs. D. O. Harton, Jr., Arkansas.

Velvet Ice Cream
(Makes 4 quarts)

1 qt. milk
2 cups brown sugar

2 tbs. cornstarch
4 egg yolks, beaten
¼ tsp. salt
½ tsp. maple flavoring
4 egg whites, stiffly beaten
2 cups heavy cream, whipped

Heat the milk to scalding. Mix the sugar with the cornstarch and egg yolks. Gradually add the scalded milk and cook until the mixture begins to thicken, stirring constantly. Remove from stove, add salt and flavoring, and set aside to cool. Fold egg whites and whipped cream into the cooled custard and freeze.

Mrs. M. J. Cook, Iowa.

Vanilla Ice Cream
(Makes 2 quarts)

2 eggs
2 cups milk
¾ cup sugar
1 tbs. vanilla
¼ tsp. salt
1 cup heavy whipping cream

Separate the eggs and make a soft custard of the milk, egg yolks, and sugar. Beat the egg whites stiff and over them pour the hot custard and mix thoroughly. Add the vanilla and salt and, when cold, the whipped cream. Freeze.

Vanilla Ice Cream Variations

1. Add ½ cup chopped dates and 1 cup chopped walnuts.

2. Add 1 small bottle maraschino cherries run through the food chopper with about half the liquid.

3. Caramelize to golden brown half the sugar used in making the custard, and add to the hot milk before adding the egg yolks.

4. Add 1 cup any well-mashed fresh fruit.

5. Add 2 tbs. orange marmalade.

6. Add 1 cup Grape-Nuts.

7. Add 1 cup chocolate cookie crumbs or 1 cup almond macaroon crumbs.

8. Add 2 squares melted chocolate to the custard foundation.

Mrs. Stephen K. Perry, Vermont.

Vanilla Ice Cream
(Makes 2 quarts)

2 eggs
1 cup milk
¼ cup sugar
¼ cup white corn syrup
2 tsp. vanilla
1 cup whipping cream

Scald the milk, separate the eggs, and add the egg yolks mixed with the sugar. Add the corn syrup and cook until the mixture coats the spoon. When cool add the 2 egg whites beaten stiff, the vanilla, and the whipped cream. Freeze.

Mrs. C. F. Hagins, Texas.

Wintermint Ice Cream
(Makes 2 quarts)

1 cup condensed milk

¾ cup water
1 tsp. green vegetable coloring
3 tbs. essence of wintergreen (unless very strong, then use only 1 tbs.)
1⅓ cups whipping cream

Mix the condensed milk, water, coloring, and flavoring and chill thoroughly. Whip the cream to the thickness of custard and fold into the chilled mixture. Freeze.

MOUSSES

Butter Brickle Mousse
(Makes 1½ quarts)

½ lb. butter brickle candy, or
½ lb. toffee
1 pt. whipping cream

Put the candy through a food chopper, using the coarse knife. Whip the cream until it holds its shape. Fold in the ground candy. Freeze.

Cherry and Orange Mousse
(Makes 2 quarts)

6 oranges
1 lemon
1 cup sugar syrup, hot
1 tsp. powdered gelatine
¾ cup cherries, diced
3 cups heavy cream

Add strained juice of oranges and lemon to sugar syrup with gelatine dissolved in the sugar syrup, add cherries and, when cold, add whipped cream. Freeze.

Chocolate Mousse
(Makes 2 quarts)

6 tbs. grated bitter chocolate
1 cup milk
1 tbs. gelatine
1 tsp. powdered cinnamon

1½ cups confectioners' sugar
2½ cups heavy cream
1 tbs. vanilla
2 tbs. cold water

Scald milk, chocolate, and sugar to almost boiling. Soak gelatine in the cold water and add to hot mixture. When cold and slightly thickened, flavor with cinnamon and vanilla. Fold in whipped cream. Freeze.

Fruit Mousse
(Makes 2 quarts)

1 lb. white grapes
¼ lb. candied pineapple
¼ lb. marshmallows
1 cup whipping cream
Pinch of salt

Skin and seed grapes, cut in half. Cut candied pineapple in thin, small slices. Cut marshmallows in fourths. Add salt to slightly-whipped cream and fold in grapes, pineapple, and marshmallows. Freeze.

Coffee Mousse
(Makes 1 quart)

½ cup coffee, double strength
¾ cup sugar
1½ cups whipped cream

Scald coffee and sugar to almost boiling. Fold in whipped cream. Freeze.

Ginger Mousse
(Makes 1½ quarts)

1 tsp. gelatine
1 tbs. cold water

1 cup milk
¼ cup finely-chopped preserved ginger
2 tbs. ginger syrup
⅓ cup sugar
⅛ tsp. salt
2 tsp. vanilla
½ pt. whipping cream

Soak the gelatine in the cold water. Dissolve over hot water and slowly add the milk, preserved ginger, chopped very fine, and remaining ingredients, except the whipping cream; mix and chill. Whip the cream until stiff and gradually fold in the gelatine mixture. Freeze.

Maple Mousse
(Makes 2 quarts)

1½ cups maple syrup
1 cup milk
1 tbs. cold water
2½ cups heavy cream
1 tbs. powdered gelatine
½ cup chopped nuts

Mix the syrup and milk, add gelatine which has been soaked in cold water and then dissolved over boiling water. Fold in cream whipped stiff. Freeze.

Peach Mousse
(Makes 2 quarts)

1½ cups crushed peach pulp
2¼ cups heavy cream
1 tbs. powdered gelatine
2 cups confectioners' sugar
1 cup milk
2 tbs. cold water

Mix milk, sugar, and peach pulp, add gelatine which has been soaked a few minutes in the cold water and dissolved over boiling water. Fold in cream whipped stiff. Freeze.

Raspberry Mousse
(Makes 2 quarts)

1 pt. raspberries
¾ cup sugar
1½ cups whipping cream

Force berries through a sieve, add sugar, and cook until berry mixture thickens, stirring frequently. Cool. Fold in whipped cream. Freeze.

Mint Mousse
(Makes 2 quarts)

1 tsp. gelatine
2 tbs. cold water
1 cup milk
½ lb. peppermint, lime, or wintergreen candies, crushed
⅛ tsp. salt
Fruit coloring (red or green)
2 cups whipping cream

Soak the gelatine in the cold water 5 minutes. Heat the milk and then dissolve the gelatine in it. Add the finely-crushed candies and the salt. Cool and add coloring, if desired—delicate green if peppermint or lime is used, red if wintergreen mints are used. Fold in cream whipped until thick. Freeze.

Mrs. J. E. Wise, Ohio.

Strawberry Mousse
(Makes 2 quarts)

1 qt. strawberries
1 to 1¼ cups sugar
1½ cups whipping cream

Mash and force the berries through a coarse sieve. Add sugar and cook until mixture begins to thicken, stirring mixture frequently toward the last of the cooking period. Cool. Fold in whipped cream and freeze.

Strawberry Mousse
(Makes 2 quarts)

2½ cups heavy cream
2 cups confectioners' sugar
2 cups crushed strawberries
1 tbs. powdered gelatine
2 tbs. cold water

Crush strawberries and press through a sieve, add sugar and gelatine which has been softened in the cold water and dissolved over boiling water. When mixture is cold and slightly thickened, fold in cream whipped stiff. Freeze.

Toasted Cocoanut Mousse
(Makes 2 quarts)

Brown lightly 1 cup of cocoanut either in the oven or under a broiler. Chill thoroughly and add to the Vanilla Ice Cream Mixture before freezing.

SHERBETS

Apricot Sherbet
(Makes 2 quarts)

Peel the skins from 1 can of apricots, then mash through a sieve. Add the apricot juice, the juice of 1 lemon and 1 orange, 1 cup sugar, and 1 cup water to the apricot pulp. Freeze to a mush and add one egg white (stiffly beaten), mix thoroughly, and continue freezing.

Mrs. H. Adams, Maryland.

Apricot Sherbet
(Makes 2 quarts)

1 qt. apricots
2½ cups sugar
1 egg (white only)
8 cups water
½ cup lemon juice
1 tsp. powdered gelatine

Wash apricots, crack and remove a few kernels from pits, put these with apricots and cook in the water until the fruit is soft. When cool, press through a sieve and measure 5 cups of juice and pulp; add sugar, lemon juice, and gelatine which has been dissolved by soaking in a tbs. cold water and then over boiling water. Whip white of egg until stiff and add. Freeze. (Peaches or other fruit may be used in place of apricots, sweetened to taste.)

Banana Sherbet
(Makes 2 quarts)

1 cup water

1½ cups sugar
6 medium-sized bananas
2 cups orange juice
2 tbs. lemon juice
1 egg white

Combine water and sugar and boil until sugar is dissolved. Cool thoroughly. Peel bananas and press through ricer. Add orange and lemon juice and combine with sugar syrup. Beat egg white slightly and add to the mixture. Freeze.

Cranberry Sherbet
(Makes 1½ quarts)

2 cups cranberries
2 cups sugar
2 cups milk
1 cup cream
3 tbs. lemon juice

Wash and cook cranberries in water until tender. Press through potato ricer, then add sugar, and cook until sugar dissolves; then chill well. Add lemon juice, milk, and cream, and pour into freezer.

Economy Sherbet
(Makes 1½ quarts)

1 pkg. orange-flavored gelatine
2 cups boiling water
¼ cup lemon juice
½ cup sugar
2 egg whites, beaten stiff

Dissolve the flavored gelatine in the boiling water and add the lemon juice and sugar. Cool. Fold in the egg whites, beaten stiff. Freeze.

Mrs. H. G. Damon, Vermont.

Favorite Sherbet
(Makes 2 quarts)

3¼ cups sugar
3 cups water
Juice of 3 lemons
Juice of 3 oranges
3 ripe bananas, crushed
3 egg whites, beaten stiff

Mix the sugar and water and boil 5 minutes, then cool. Add the juice of the lemons and oranges, then the crushed bananas. Freeze to a mush and then fold in the stiffly-beaten egg whites and continue freezing until firm.

Mrs. J. A. Badgley, Illinois.

Fruit Sherbet
(Makes 2 quarts)

3 cups sugar
3 pts. water
Juice of 3 lemons
Juice of 3 oranges
3 bananas, sliced thin
1 No. 2 can crushed pineapple
1 egg white, beaten stiff

Mix the sugar and water and cook 5 minutes. Cool slightly and add the fruit juices and the fruit. Pour in ice-cream freezer and add the stiffly-beaten egg white. Freeze.

Mrs. B. L. Parham, Indiana.

Glenridge Sherbet
(Makes 2 quarts)

4 cups water

1 cup sugar
1 tbs. gelatine
4 tbs. cold water
2 tbs. finely-chopped fresh mint
Juice of 4 lemons

Make a syrup of sugar and water. Dissolve the gelatine in 4 tbs. cold water. Combine the two and add lemon juice and chopped mint. Freeze.

Grape Sherbet
(Makes 1 quart)

20 marshmallows
1 cup grape juice
2 tbs. orange juice
4 tbs. lemon juice
¼ cup egg whites
1 tbs. sugar

Place marshmallows and grape juice in a double boiler and heat together, stirring frequently until the marshmallows are melted. Remove and add the fruit juices, and chill. Beat the egg whites and sugar together, fold thoroughly into the jellied grape mixture, and freeze.

Mrs. M. Spruill, Colorado.

Grapefruit Sherbet
(Makes 2 quarts)

4 grapefruits
3 cups water
2 eggs (whites only)
1½ cups sugar
1 cup orange or other fruit juice

Boil together for 10 minutes the water and sugar. When cold, add strained juice of grapefruits, or enough to measure 3 cups; add orange or fruit juices.

Whip whites of eggs and add to mixture. Freeze.

Lemon Cream Sherbet
(Makes 1 quart)

⅓ cup lemon juice
1½ cups milk
½ cup thin cream
⅛ tsp. salt
2 tsp. gelatine
¼ cup cold water
⅓ cup sugar
⅓ cup white corn syrup
1 tsp. grated lemon rind

Soak the gelatine in the cold water and dissolve over hot water. Mix together the remaining ingredients and add gradually to the gelatine mixture. Freeze.

Mrs. R. H. Otto, Connecticut.

Lemon Milk Sherbet
(Makes 1½ quarts)

One quart of milk, two cups of sugar, juice of three lemons. Dissolve the sugar in the milk and partly freeze before adding the strained lemon juice. Crushed or preserved fruit served with the sherbet adds much to the deliciousness.

Lime Sherbet
(Makes 1½ quarts)

20 marshmallows
1 cup boiling water
1 cup ginger ale
¼ cup fresh lime juice

1 tsp. lemon juice
Green vegetable coloring
1 tbs. sugar
2 egg whites

Melt the marshmallows in the boiling water. Add the ginger ale, fruit juices, and coloring, and cool. Add the sugar to the beaten egg whites, beat, and combine with the lime mixture. Freeze.

Mrs. W. N. Hubbard, Massachusetts.

Orange Cream Sherbet
(Makes 1½ quarts)

1 cup orange juice
1 tbs. lemon juice
½ cup evaporated milk
1 egg white
1 tsp. gelatine
1 tbs. cold water
¾ cup sugar
¼ cup water
1 tsp. grated orange rind

Soak the gelatine in the tbs. of cold water for 5 minutes, and soften over boiling water. Boil the sugar, water, and orange rind together and strain into softened gelatine. Add the fruit juices and cool.

When thoroughly chilled, whip the evaporated milk and egg white separately and combine. Then fold slowly into the fruit and gelatine mixture and freeze. (To whip evaporated milk, chill it throughly; then whip until it is thick.)

Mrs. L. Estes, California.

Orange Fruit Sherbet
(Makes 2 quarts)

1 cup sugar
2 tbs. lemon juice
½ cup cream
2 cups orange pulp and juice
1½ cups water

Boil sugar and water for 10 minutes, and then cool. Cut oranges in halves, crosswise, and carefully remove pulp in pieces, together with remaining juice. Measure 2 cups and add lemon juice. Combine with cold sugar syrup. Freeze to a soft mush and fold into the sherbet the cream which has been whipped. Re-cover freezer and freeze stiff.

Orange Pineapple Sherbet
(Makes 4 quarts)

2 cups sugar
2 cups water
1 cup crushed pineapple and juice
1 bottle orange crush
Juice of 1 lemon
2 cups whole milk

Boil the sugar and water for 5 minutes. Remove from the stove and set aside to cool. Add the remaining ingredients and mix thoroughly. Freeze.

Mrs. B. Knight, Tennessee.

Pineapple Sherbet
(Makes 2 quarts)

¾ cup sugar
1½ cups water
1 tbs. gelatine
¼ cup cold water
½ cup pineapple juice
Juice of 1 lemon
Juice of ½ orange
1 cup shredded pineapple, drained
⅛ tsp. salt
2 egg whites
½ cup whipping cream

Boil the sugar and water together 5 minutes. Add the gelatine which has been soaked in the cold water 5 minutes. When cool, add the fruit juices and pineapple. Freeze. Add the salt to the egg whites and beat stiff. Whip the cream until thick but not stiff and combine with the partially-frozen mixture; then fold in the egg whites and continue freezing.

Mrs. C. M. Tichacek, Nebraska.

Pineapple Cream Sherbet
(Makes 1½ quarts)

3 cups grated fresh pineapple
1½ cups sugar
2 cups cream

Cover pineapple with sugar (for canned pineapple use 1 cup only) and let stand three hours. Add the cream. Freeze.

Raspberry Sherbet
(Makes 1½ quarts)

1 pt. red raspberries
½ cup water
½ cup whipping cream

¾ cup sugar
2 tbs. lemon juice
1 egg white

Put the fresh berries in a saucepan with the water and sugar and cook for 5 minutes. Press through a sieve and add the lemon juice. With canned berries omit the water. Simply heat in their own juice and press through a sieve. Cool. Beat until light and then fold in the egg white, beaten stiff, and beat the mixture again. Fold in the cream whipped until thick and stir well. Freeze.

Mrs. R. H. Otto, Connecticut.

PUDDINGS AND BISQUES

Alaska Pudding

1½ cups orange juice
1 tsp. vanilla
⅔ cup chopped almonds
¼ cup lemon juice
1½ cups powdered sugar
1 pt. heavy cream

Blanch almonds and brown them in the oven before chopping. Mix the fruit juices with half of the sugar and let stand until sugar is thoroughly dissolved. Whip the cream, adding the rest of the sugar, the vanilla, and the chopped nuts. Pour over the first mixture. Freeze.

Chocolate Raisin Pudding

2½ cups milk
1¼ cups sugar
2 squares bitter chocolate, grated
Juice and grated rind of 1 lemon
1 tbs. vanilla
1 tbs. arrowroot
2 cups cream
1 cup chopped seedless raisins
2 eggs
⅛ tsp. salt

Scald milk and stir slowly over the beaten eggs, sugar, arrowroot, salt, grated melted chocolate, and chopped raisins. Cook mixture in a double boiler, stirring constantly until it thickens. When cold, add cream, juice, and rind of lemon and vanilla. Freeze.

Frozen Caramel Pudding

1 can condensed milk
1 cup whipping cream
1 tsp. vanilla
½ cup chopped maraschino cherries
½ cup crushed nut meats

Cover the can of condensed milk with boiling water and boil 3 hours. Remove and chill thoroughly. Whip the cream until thick but not stiff and gradually add the caramelized milk, thoroughly mixing it into the cream. Flavor with the vanilla and add the maraschino cherries and nut meats. Freeze.

Frozen Custard

1½ qts. scalded milk
½ cup sugar
Few grains salt
2 tbs. cornstarch
1 egg
1 tbs. vanilla

Mix together ¼ cup sugar, cornstarch, and a few grains of salt. Pour the scalded milk over this mixture and return to the double boiler. Cook 20 minutes. Beat the egg until light and add ¼ cup sugar. Pour the hot milk mixture over it, stirring constantly. Return to double boiler and cook 3 minutes longer. Remove from stove, thoroughly chill, and add vanilla. Freeze.

Frozen Custard with Marrons

2 cups diced marrons
Maraschino syrup
4 cups milk
6 egg yolks
⅔ cup sugar
1 tsp. salt
1 tbs. vanilla

Cut the marrons into small pieces and cover 2 cups with maraschino syrup. Let stand for 1 hour. Scald 4 cups milk in a double boiler, beat the egg yolks, and add sugar and salt and beat again. Dilute with a little of the hot milk, mix thoroughly, and stir in the balance of the milk. Stir and cook until mixture coats the spoon slightly. Strain. Add vanilla. Chill and freeze. When the mixture begins to harden, open freezer and stir in 2 cups of marrons. Freeze hard.

Frozen Plum Pudding

½ cup milk
½ cup sugar
2 sqs. chocolate, grated
2 cups whipping cream
1 cup chopped raisins
¼ cup chopped dates or figs
½ cup finely-chopped nut meats
¼ cup maraschino cherries, chopped
1 tsp. vanilla

Put the milk in a saucepan, add the sugar and grated chocolate, and cook until the chocolate is melted and the mixture slightly thick. Chill. Whip the cream until thick but not stiff, add the chilled chocolate mixture, vanilla, fruits, and freeze.

(Note: The raisins and dates should be cooked in a small amount of water which is allowed to evaporate, then chopped and added to the mixture. The nut meats may be omitted.)

Marshmallow Pudding

½ lb. marshmallows
Milk or cream to cover
½ pt. double cream
Ground walnut meats

Cut marshmallows to fourths. Cover with milk or cream and soak 5 hours. Freeze, but do not freeze solid. Whip the cream and serve over frozen marshmallows, sprinkling with ground walnuts.

Mexican Frozen Pudding

1½ cups milk
1 cup brown sugar
2 eggs
12 maraschino cherries, chopped
¼ cup English walnut meats, chopped
1 cup whipping cream

Scald milk, add sugar. Pour over slightly-beaten eggs. Cook on LOW until consistency of thin custard, stirring frequently. Cool. Fold in whipped cream, cherries, and nuts. Freeze.

Pineapple Pudding

3 cups milk
2 cups grated canned pineapple
¼ cup grated cocoanut
1 tsp. lemon extract
1½ cups cream
4 egg yolks
1 cup sugar
1 tbs. arrowroot
¼ tsp. salt

Scald milk and stir into well-beaten eggs, sugar, salt, and arrowroot. Cook mixture in double boiler, stirring constantly until it thickens. Remove from fire and when cold add cream, pineapple, cocoanut, and lemon extract. Freeze.

Macaroon Date Bisque

2 cups heavy cream
4 eggs
1 doz. macaroons (crushed fine)
1 tbs. lemon juice
1 cup milk
¾ cup sugar
½ cup dates (chopped fine)
½ tsp. almond extract
⅛ tsp. salt

Scald milk and stir slowly over well-beaten eggs and sugar. Dry macaroons in hot oven and crush fine, stir into mixture; add chopped, seeded dates, lemon juice, almond extract, and salt. Fold in the cream whipped stiff. Freeze.

Macaroon Orange Bisque

1 cup milk
2 cups cream
1 cup powdered macaroons
¼ cup candied orange peel
4 egg yolks
1 cup sugar
1 cup orange juice and pulp
1 tsp. orange extract
⅛ tsp. salt

Scald milk and stir slowly over well-beaten eggs and sugar. Dry macaroons in oven and roll or crush to a powder, add to mixture; add orange juice and pulp, candied orange peel, chopped fine, orange extract, and salt. Fold in cream whipped stiff. Freeze.

Pineapple Bisque

4 egg yolks
1¼ cups sugar
2 cups whipping cream
4 tbs. cake crumbs
1 small can grated pineapple
1 cup orange juice

Beat yolks of eggs with sugar until thick, add cream whipped, crumbs, pineapple, and orange juice. Freeze.

Pistachio Bisque

4 cups cream
1 cup powdered macaroons
½ cup peanuts (chopped fine)
½ cup almonds (chopped fine)
1 tsp. vanilla extract
½ cup pistachio nuts (chopped fine)
1 tsp. pistachio extract
Few drops green vegetable coloring
1 cup confectioners sugar

Dissolve sugar in cream, add powdered macaroons, chopped nuts, extracts, and green coloring. Freeze. Serve with lemon cream sauce, if desired.

PARFAITS

Angel Parfait

1 cup sugar
¼ cup water
3 egg whites
2 cups whipping cream
1 tbs. vanilla

Boil the sugar and water until the syrup will thread when dropped from a fork. Pour slowly over the egg whites, beaten stiff, and beat until fluffy. Let cool and add the cream, whipped, and the vanilla. Freeze.

Banana and Browned Almond Parfait

1 tbs. gelatine
2 tbs. cold water
6 ripe bananas
½ cup powdered sugar
Few grains salt
2 tbs. lemon juice
¾ cup almonds
2 cups cream

Soak gelatine in water 5 minutes and dissolve over boiling water. Put bananas through potato ricer, add sugar, salt, lemon juice, and dissolved gelatine. Add almonds which have been browned in oven and crushed fine. Let mixture stand until it begins to congeal, then fold in stiffly-beaten cream. Freeze.

Caramel Parfait

1 cup sugar
½ cup water
2 cups cream, whipped
1 tbs. vanilla
6 egg yolks

Caramelize one-half cup sugar. Add the water slowly and stir until dissolved. Add the remaining one-half cup sugar and cook until mixture threads. Pour slowly over beaten egg yolks. Cook in the top of a double boiler until the mixture thickens. Cool. Then fold in the cream which has been beaten stiff. Add vanilla and pour into mold. Freeze.

Caramel Coffee Parfait

½ cup brown sugar
2 cups evaporated milk
2 cups heavy cream
4 egg yolks
2 tbs. powdered coffee
½ cup water
¾ cup granulated sugar
1 tsp. vanilla

Caramelize brown sugar. Scald coffee, evaporated milk, and water to boiling point and stir in caramelized sugar; when sugar is dissolved, strain and stir the mixture slowly into well-beaten yolks of eggs and granulated sugar. Cook in double boiler, stirring constantly until it thickens. Remove from fire and, when cold, add the vanilla and cream whipped stiff. Freeze.

Chocolate Parfait

¾ cup sugar
¾ cup water
3 egg whites
2 ozs. bitter chocolate, grated and melted
1 tsp. vanilla

1½ cups whipping cream

Cook sugar and water until syrup spins a long thread. Gradually pour over stiffly-beaten egg whites, beating until COLD. Add vanilla and melted chocolate that has been cooled. Fold in whipped cream. Freeze.

Chocolate Parfait

6 tbs. grated bitter chocolate
4 eggs
1 cup thin cream or evaporated milk
1¼ cups sugar
2½ cups heavy cream
1 tsp. vanilla
½ tsp. cinnamon

Dissolve chocolate over boiling water and stir into it thin cream or evaporated milk and well-beaten eggs and sugar. Cook in double boiler until mixture thickens. Strain and, when cold, flavor with vanilla and cinnamon. Add cream, whipped stiff. Freeze.

Coffee Parfait

1 cup milk
¼ cup coffee
3 egg yolks
⅛ tsp. salt
1 cup sugar
3 cups cream

Heat milk and coffee together. Beat egg yolks and add sugar and salt. Pour milk and coffee slowly on this mixture and cook until slightly thickened. Cool, add cream, and freeze.

Coffee Parfait

⅔ cup sugar
½ cup coffee, double strength
2 egg whites
1 tsp. vanilla
1½ cups whipping cream

Boil sugar and coffee until the syrup spins a long thread. Cool. Add vanilla and fold in whipped cream. Freeze.

Fruit Parfait

1¾ cups sugar
4 egg yolks
½ cup grated pineapple
½ cup orange juice and pulp
1 tsp. extract
½ cup water
2½ cups cream
¼ cup lemon juice
½ cup maraschino cherries (cut fine)

Boil sugar and water 5 minutes. Stir into well-beaten eggs when mixture is cold, add fruit and juice. Whip cream stiff and fold in. Freeze.

Golden Parfait

1 cup sugar
½ cup water
2 cups cream, whipped
1 tbs. vanilla
6 egg yolks

Boil sugar and water slowly until it threads. Pour slowly over beaten egg yolks. Cook in the top of a double boiler until the mixture thickens. Cool. Then fold in the cream which has been beaten stiff. Add vanilla and pour into mold. Freeze.

Hawaiian Delight Parfait

1 can sliced pineapple
4 eggs
5 tbs. sugar
1 pt. heavy cream

Out of 1 can Hawaiian pineapple prepare ½ cup finely-chopped fruit, leaving remaining slices to line a 2-qt. mold. Beat the egg yolks until very light, add sugar, and mix with ¾ cup pineapple syrup. Stir over fire until as thick as cream, then remove from heat and add chopped pineapple. When cold, whip the cream solid, fold two mixtures together, pour into mold, and freeze.

Lemon Parfait

1½ cups sugar
4 egg whites
1 tsp. lemon extract
½ cup water
½ cup lemon juice
2 cups cream

Boil sugar and water to a thick syrup. Whip eggs to a stiff froth, beat the syrup over the eggs slowly, add lemon juice and extract; cool, fold in cream whipped stiff. Freeze.

Maple Parfait

1¼ cups maple syrup
2½ cups heavy cream
4 eqgs
1 cup chopped pecans

Heat maple syrup and stir slowly into beaten eggs. Whip cream stiff and add. Partially freeze, then stir in thoroughly the pecans chopped very fine.

Finish freezing.

Maple Nut Parfait

¾ cup maple syrup
4 egg yolks
1 cup whipping cream
½ cup chopped English walnut meats

Boil syrup 5 minutes. Beat egg yolks until light and lemon colored. Pour syrup gradually over the beaten egg yolks, beating constantly. Cook on LOW heat until thick. Cool. Fold in whipped cream and lastly the nuts. Freeze.

Peach Parfait

1 cup mashed fresh or canned peaches
1 cup sugar
⅓ cup water
2 egg whites
Juice of 1 orange
1 pt. heavy cream, whipped
Few drops bitter almond

Boil sugar (if canned peaches are used, reduce amount of sugar to ¾ cup) and water together until it threads, and pour gently into the egg whites which have been beaten stiff, whipping constantly. Combine the peaches and orange juice. Beat in the egg-white mixture. Stir briskly until cool and then fold in the whipped cream and almond, which should be used sparingly. Pour into mold and freeze.

Pineapple Parfait

1 can sliced pineapple
4 egg yolks

5 tbs. sugar
1 tsp. gelatine
1 tbs. cold water
1 pt. heavy cream

Beat egg yolks light—add sugar and mix with ¾ cup pineapple juice. Stir over fire until thick as cream. Remove from fire and add gelatine which has been soaked for 5 minutes in cold water. Add pineapple and cool. Fold into cream and freeze.

Plain Parfait

⅔ cup sugar
½ cup water
2 eggs
1 tsp. vanilla
1½ cups whipping cream

Boil water and sugar until the syrup spins a thread. Beat egg yolks until light lemon colored. Gradually pour hot syrup over beaten egg yolks, beating constantly, then pour mixture gradually over stiffly-beaten egg whites, beating all the time. Cool. Add flavoring and fold in whipped cream. Freeze.

Maple Parfait

4 eggs
1 cup hot maple syrup
1 pt. cream

Beat eggs and pour maple syrup on them slowly. Cook until it thickens and add cream beaten until stiff. Freeze.

FRAPPÉS AND ICES

Apricot Frappé

1 cup sugar
½ cup white corn syrup
4 tbs. lemon juice
2 cups apricot pulp and juice
2 cups water

Cook syrup, 1 cup of water, and sugar together until mixture threads. Remove from fire and add lemon juice, one cup of water, and the canned or cooked apricots which have been mashed through a coarse sieve. Cool. Freeze.

Banana Frappé

1 cup sugar
6 tbs. pectin
2 cups water
2 bananas
1 cup orange juice
2 tbs. lemon juice

Boil sugar and 1 cup water, add liquid pectin. Remove from fire and add 1 cup water, orange and lemon juice, and the bananas which have been mashed through a coarse sieve. Cool. Freeze.

Coffee Frappé

7 cups clear coffee
1 cup sugar

Dissolve sugar with coffee and partially freeze. Serve in tall glasses with a tablespoon of whipped cream on top.

Fruit Frappé

    4 cups cider
    1 cup peach or apricot juice (canned)
    1½ cups sugar
    1 cup orange juice
    1 cup pineapple (canned)
    ¼ cup lemon juice

Stir fruit juice with sugar until the sugar is dissolved. Freeze.

Grape Juice Frappé

    1½ cups sugar
    3¼ cups water
    ¾ cup white corn syrup
    3 tbs. pectin
    6 tbs. lemon juice
    1½ cups grape juice

Combine sugar, 1 cup water, syrup, and pectin and cook to boiling. Remove from fire, add lemon juice, grape juice, and 2¼ cups water. Cool and freeze.

Grape Juice Frappé

    1 qt. grape juice
    3 cups water
    ½ cup lemon juice
    1 cup sugar

Boil water and sugar 5 minutes; add lemon juice and grape juice. Freeze.

Orange Frappé

1½ cups sugar
¾ cup white corn syrup
6 tbs. lemon juice
3 cups orange juice
1¾ cups water

Cook syrup, 1 cup water and sugar together until mixture threads. Remove from fire and add fruit juices and ¾ cup water. Chill. Freeze.

Orange Frappé

3½ cups water
2 cups sugar
3 cups orange juice
½ cup lemon juice

Grate rinds of three oranges and one lemon into sugar, add water, and boil five minutes. When cold add fruit juice. Freeze.

Pineapple Frappé

4 cups canned grated pineapple
2 cups sugar
3 cups water
½ cup lemon juice
1 tsp. pineapple extract

Boil water and sugar for 10 minutes. Pour the hot syrup over pineapple. When cold, add lemon juice and pineapple extract. Freeze.

Raspberry Frappé

2 qts. raspberries

1 qt. water
3 tbs. lemon juice
3¼ cups sugar

Press berries through sieve. Boil sugar and water together until sugar is dissolved. Cool. Add raspberry juice and lemon juice. Freeze.

Spiced Grapefruit Frappé

½ cup water
2 tbs. sugar
3 whole cloves
3½-inch sticks cinnamon
3 cups grape juice

Combine the water, sugar, and spices and boil 5 minutes. Cool, add to the grape juice and freeze until the frappé stage is reached, or about 3 hours. Stir at the end of the first 30 minutes and at intervals thereafter.

Mrs. D. N. Magruder, New Mexico.

Strawberry Frappé

2 qts. strawberries
4 cups water
2½ cups sugar

Boil sugar and water for 5 minutes; wash and press strawberries through a sieve; measure 3 cups juice and pulp, add to syrup. Freeze.

Strawberry Frappé

1½ cups sugar
¾ cup white corn syrup
1½ cups fresh mashed strawberries
3 tbs. liquid pectin

8 tbs. lemon juice
¾ cup water

Cook sugar, syrup, and pectin together. Remove from heat and add lemon juice and strawberries which have been mashed and put through a sieve. Add water. Cool. Freeze.

Creme de Menthe Ice

2 cups sugar
1 qt. water
½ cup creme de menthe syrup
¾ cup lemon juice
⅛ tsp. salt

Make a syrup by boiling the sugar and water together, cool, and add the remaining ingredients. Freeze.

Mrs. H. L. Oliver, Florida.

Ginger Ale Ice

1 cup sugar
1 cup water
¼ cup lemon juice
1 tsp. grated lemon rind
¼ cup pineapple juice
1 pt. bottle ginger ale

Mix sugar, water, and lemon rind. Boil 5 minutes. Cool. Add lemon juice and pineapple juice. Freeze.

Grape Juice Ice

¾ cup sugar
1 cup water

2 tbs. lemon juice
¼ cup orange juice
2 cups grape juice
2 tsp. gelatine

Boil sugar and water 5 minutes. Add gelatine that has been soaked in ¼ cup grape juice for 5 minutes, stirring until gelatine is dissolved. Cool. Add lemon juice, orange juice, and grape juice. Freeze.

Lemon Ice

4 cups water
2 cups sugar
¾ cup lemon juice

Boil water and sugar to make syrup, add lemon juice. Freeze.

Lemon Water Ice

6 cups water
2 cups sugar
3 lemons
2 oranges
½ tsp. lemon extract

Boil water, sugar, grated rinds of oranges and lemons for eight minutes, then strain and cool. When cold, add strained juice of lemons, oranges, and extract. Freeze.

Mint Ice

1¼ cups sugar
1 cup water
1 cup grapefruit juice
1 cup pineapple juice
2 tbs. lemon juice

¼ tsp. essence peppermint
Green coloring

Boil sugar and water 5 minutes. Cool. Add grapefruit juice, pineapple juice, lemon juice, peppermint, and green coloring. Freeze.

Orange Ice

3½ cups water
2 cups sugar
3 cups orange juice
½ cup lemon juice

Grate rinds of three oranges and one lemon into sugar, add water, and boil 5 minutes. When cold, add fruit juice. Freeze.

Orange Ice

1 cup sugar
½ cup water
1 tsp. grated orange rind
¼ cup lemon juice
2 cups orange juice
¼ cup water
1 tsp. gelatine

Mix sugar, water, and orange rind; boil 5 minutes. Cool. Allow gelatine to soak in ¼ cup water several minutes. Dissolve and add to sugar syrup with orange juice and lemon juice. Freeze.

Pear Ice

Drain the juice from a can of pears. Mash the pears and add the juice, which should measure about 1¼ cups. Add the same amount (1¼ cups) ginger ale. Stir thoroughly. Freeze.

Strawberry Ice

1 qt. strawberries
1 cup water
¾ cup sugar
2 tbs. lemon juice

Force berries through a sieve, add sugar and water, cook until sugar is dissolved and berries begin to puff, which is just before boiling point is reached. Add lemon juice. Cool. Freeze.

SAUCES

Caramel Sauce

1½ cups sugar
1 cup water
1 tsp. vanilla

Caramelize sugar and stir in slowly the boiling water. Let boil to a thick syrup, add vanilla. If the sauce is to be served hot, let the saucepan containing it remain in a large pan of hot water until needed. Chopped seedless raisins may be added to this sauce.

Chocolate Sauce

3 sqs. bitter chocolate
1 cup evaporated milk
1 cup powdered sugar
½ cup water
1 tsp. vanilla

Cut chocolate into small pieces and melt in a pan over boiling water. Stir in the sugar, evaporated milk, and water until sugar is dissolved. Place over fire and cook slowly without stirring until a little dropped into cold water may be rolled into a soft ball. Flavor with vanilla. Keep the sauce warm by placing over a pan of hot water until ready to serve.

Fruit Sauce

Make syrup as for nut sauce and add a cup of crushed strawberries or other fruits; leave out nuts.

Hot Maple Sauce

2 cups maple syrup
1 tsp. melted butter
1 cup thin cream or evaporated milk
½ cup chopped walnut meats or pecans

Mix maple syrup, butter, and cream. Cook slowly without stirring until a little dropped into cold water may be rolled into a soft ball. Keep warm over a pan of hot water until ready to serve. Sprinkle top of each dish with nuts, chopped fine.

Lemon Cream Sauce

1 cup heavy cream
1 egg white
⅛ tsp. nutmeg
6 tbs. confectioners' sugar
1 tbs. lemon juice
⅛ tsp. salt

Whip cream and white of egg, add sugar, lemon juice, nutmeg, and salt. Serve over any flavor of ice cream or sherbets.

Marshmallow Sauce

½ lb. marshmallows
½ tsp. orange extract
1 cup confectioners' sugar
½ cup hot water

Cut marshmallows into small pieces and dissolve in top of double boiler and add sugar and boiling water and heat thoroughly; add orange extract. Let cool and serve.

Medium White Sauce

6 tbs. butter
6 tbs. flour
3 cups scalded milk

Melt butter, add flour, and blend. Add scalded milk. Cook on LOW heat, stirring frequently until thick. Cool. Add salt and pepper just before serving.

Nut Sauce

1½ cups sugar
1 cup chopped walnut meats
½ cup water
1 tsp. vanilla
⅛ tsp. salt

Boil sugar and water to a thick syrup, add nuts, salt, and extract. Serve on ice cream, hot or cold.

Orange Sauce

4 whites of eggs
3 oranges
4 tbs. confectioners' sugar
1 tsp. lemon extract

Beat whites of eggs until stiff, add sugar and beat again, then add grated rind and strained orange juice and lemon extract. Stir the mixture well.

Thin White Sauce

6 tbs. butter
3 tbs. flour
3 cups scalded milk

Melt butter, add flour, and blend. Add scalded milk. Cook on LOW heat, stirring frequently until thick. Cool. Add salt and pepper just before stirring.

Whipped Cream Sauce

½ cup confectioners' sugar
1 cup heavy cream
1 tsp. vanilla extract

Whip cream until stiff, beat in sugar and vanilla. Chill and serve on any frozen dessert. Chopped candied fruit or nuts may be added to this sauce, or ½ cup maraschino cherries, chopped fine.

FROZEN SALADS

Chicken Salad

4 cups cooked chicken
4 cups celery
¼ cup finely-chopped sweet cucumber pickles
⅔ cup cooked salad dressing
1 tbs. lemon juice
Salt and pepper to taste
2 tbs. mayonnaise dressing

Cut chicken in ½-inch pieces and cut celery in small pieces. Mix together. Add pickles, cooked salad dressing, and lemon juice. Mix by tossing together with two forks. Add mayonnaise. Freeze.

Frozen Cheese Salad

¾ lb. roquefort cheese
1½ cups butter
1 tsp. paprika
1½ tsp. salt
⅛ tsp. red pepper
2 tbs. chopped olives or pickles or chives
1 cup cream

Shred cheese and beat it thoroughly with the butter, add the seasoning, olives, and cream. Freeze.

Frozen Cheese Salad

¼ cup scalding milk

½ lb. roquefort cheese
1 cup whipping cream
3 tbs. crushed and drained pineapple
6 chopped stuffed olives

Mash the cheese with a fork, add the scalding milk, and work to a smooth paste. Add the crushed pineapple and chopped olives, then fold in the cream whipped until it holds its shape. Freeze.

Frozen Cheese and Prune Salad

1½ cups cooked prune pulp
4 tsp. lemon juice
1½ tbs. sugar
⅓ cup finely-chopped pecans
½ cup mild American cheese, freshly grated
½ cup whipping cream

Remove the stone from cooked prunes and rub through a sieve, enough to measure 1½ cups. Add the lemon juice, sugar, and pecans. Fold the grated cheese into the cream whipped but not stiff. Freeze.

Frozen Fruit Salad

1 cup grated canned pineapple
1 cup white grapes (Seeds removed and chopped fine)
1 cup sliced bananas
1 tsp. salt
½ cup powdered sugar
1 cup orange juice and pulp
¼ cup lemon juice
1 cup apples (chopped fine)
½ cup English walnuts (chopped fine)
2 tbs. powdered gelatine

Mix the fruit, celery, and nuts. Season with salt and sugar. Add gelatine which has been softened in 2 tbs. cold water and dissolved over boiling water. Freeze.

Frozen Fruit Salad

    4 beaten egg yolks
    ¼ cup sugar
    ¼ cup vinegar or lemon juice
    ⅛ tsp. salt
    2 cups whipping cream

Mix the beaten egg yolks with the sugar, add the vinegar or lemon juice and salt, and cook in a double boiler until thick, stirring occasionally. Cool and add the cream which has been whipped until thick. Add the following:

    3 cups diced, drained, canned pineapple
    ½ cup cut maraschino cherries
    12 marshmallows cut into pieces
    1 cup blanched and chopped almonds or other nut meats

Mix and freeze.

Frozen Tomato Salad

    7 cups tomato juice and pulp
    1 tsp. minced onion
    3 tbs. sugar
    ½ tsp. paprika
    1 tbs. vinegar
    1 tsp. salt
    ¼ tsp. black pepper

Press tomatoes through a sieve, add paprika, onion, vinegar, sugar, salt, and pepper. Let stand 1 hour. Freeze.

Frozen Vegetable Salad

1 cup cottage cheese
1 tbs. mayonnaise
1 tsp. salt
1 cup canned or diced fresh tomatoes
2 tbs. minced red pepper
2 tbs. minced green pepper
1 cup whipping cream
½ cup cooked and chopped green beans

Break up the cottage cheese and stir in the mayonnaise and salt. Run the canned tomatoes through a sieve to remove the more solid parts. Fresh tomatoes are peeled, diced quite finely, and used without draining. Add the chopped green beans and minced peppers to the cottage cheese mixture. Whip the cream and fold in last. Freeze.

Miss B. Hammer, Iowa.

MAIN DISHES

Chicken Mousse

2 cups chicken, chopped fine
2 cups heavy cream
1 tsp. salt
⅛ tsp. cayenne pepper
1 cup chicken stock
1 tbs. powdered gelatine
¼ tsp. black pepper
⅛ tsp. nutmeg
1 tbs. cold water

Chop chicken to almost a paste and press it through a sieve. Season with salt, pepper, and nutmeg. Heat chicken stock and add gelatine which has been softened in the cold water, mix with chicken. Whip cream and add. Freeze.

Chicken Mousse in Patty Shells

3 egg yolks
1 cup hot chicken stock
Salt, white pepper, paprika
1 tsp. gelatine
1 tbs. cold water
⅔ cup cooked, chopped chicken
⅓ cup minced cashew nuts
1 cup whipping cream
6 patty shells
Sliced cherries

Beat the egg yolks lightly, add the chicken stock, and cook over hot water until thick, smooth sauce is formed, stirring occasionally. Remove from the stove, and add the gelatine which has been soaked in the cold water for 5 minutes, then add the chicken and the minced cashew nuts or pecans. Cool and fold in the cream which has been whipped until thick but not stiff. Freeze.

Mrs. K. S. Scott, Washington.

Frozen Chicken Pie

- 1 tbs. butter
- 1 tbs. flour
- 1 cup milk
- 1 tbs. gelatine
- 1 tbs. cold water
- ¼ cup mayonnaise
- Salt
- 1 tbs. lemon juice
- 1½ cups cold diced chicken
- ½ cup white grapes cut in half
- ½ cup diced celery
- ½ cup blanched and chopped almonds
- ½ cup whipping cream
- 8 individual pastry shells

Melt the butter in a saucepan. Add the flour and smooth to a paste. Add the milk and stir until a thin, smooth white sauce is formed. In the meantime soak the gelatine in the cold water for 5 minutes, then add to the hot sauce and stir until the gelatine is dissolved. Cool and add the mayonnaise, lemon juice, chicken, grapes, celery, and almonds. Whip the cream until thick but not stiff, fold into the mixture, and season to taste with salt. Freeze.

Mrs. H. P. Gregory, Illinois.

Frozen Chicken a la King

Make a cream sauce of the following:

   1½ tbs. butter
   1½ tbs. flour
   ½ cup chicken stock
   2 egg yolks
   ½ cup cream or undiluted evaporated milk

When thick, remove from the heat and add the beaten yolks of the 2 eggs, return to the stove, and cook 1 minute.

Meanwhile prepare the following ingredients:

   1 cup finely-minced chicken
   ¼ cup thinly-sliced stuffed olives
   ¼ cup sliced, canned mushrooms
   ¼ cup ground nut meats, preferably almonds or cashews
   ½ cup whipping cream
   2 egg whites

Add the chicken, olives, mushrooms, and nut meats to the cream sauce, and chill. When cold, fold in the cream, whipped, then the beaten egg whites, and freeze.

Mrs. T. Lessmeister, Illinois.

Frozen Crab Meat in Tomatoes

   2 cups canned tomatoes
   2 whole cloves
   1 small onion, minced
   ½ tsp. celery seed
   1 tbs. sugar
   1 tsp. salt
   ⅛ tsp. white pepper
   1 tbs. lemon juice
   1 tbs. gelatine
   2 tbs. cold water

1 cup crab meat
3 tbs. finely-diced green pepper
1 cup whipping cream

Combine the tomatoes, cloves, onion, celery seed, sugar, salt, and white pepper, and simmer for 15 minutes. Strain, add the lemon juice and the gelatine which has been softened in the cold water for 5 minutes. Chill and, when beginning to thicken, fold in the crab meat (flaked and drained of any juice), the minced green pepper, and the whipped cream. Freeze.

Mrs. D. L. McKnight, Ohio.

Ham Mousse

1 tbs. gelatine
¼ cup cold water
¼ cup boiling water
¼ cup mayonnaise
2 cups finely-chopped cooked ham
10 ripe olives, minced fine
1½ cups whipping cream
Salt to taste
1 tsp. prepared horseradish

Soak the gelatine in the cold water for 5 minutes. Add the boiling water and stir until the gelatine is dissolved. Cool and add the mayonnaise, horseradish, ham, and olives. Fold in the cream whipped until it holds its shape. Season to taste with salt. Freeze.

Ethel Schaefer, Texas.

Ham and Chicken Mousse

3 egg yolks
1½ cups scalded milk
1 tbs. gelatine

¼ cup cold water
½ cup tomato juice
1 cup chopped cooked ham
1 cup chopped cooked chicken
½ cup finely-grated American cheese
Salt and pepper
1 tbs. chopped pimento
1 cup whipping cream

Beat the egg yolks, mix with the scalded milk, and cook in a double boiler, stirring often until the mixture thickens slightly. Soak the gelatine in the cold water for 5 minutes and dissolve in the hot tomato juice. Add to the hot custard mixture and stir until thoroughly mixed. Add the ham, chicken, cheese, pimento, salt and pepper to taste, and cool. Fold in the cream whipped until it holds its shape. Freeze.

Mrs. A. E. Taylor, West Virginia.

Rice and Chicken Luncheon Dish

1 tbs. gelatine
2 tbs. cold water
1 cup hot, well-seasoned chicken stock
2 cups cooked and drained rice
1½ cups chopped cooked chicken or fish
¼ cup finely-cut pimentos
Salt to taste
1½ cups whipped cream

Soak the gelatine in the cold water for 5 minutes. Add the hot chicken stock and stir until the gelatine is dissolved. Cool and add the rice, chicken, pimentos, and season to taste with salt. Fold in the cream which has been whipped until thick but not stiff. Freeze.

Mrs. J. A. Dresp, So. Dakota.

Tomato Mousse

3 lbs. tomatoes
1 bay leaf
1½ tsp. salt
1 tsp. pepper
3 tsp. sugar
2 cloves
½ tsp. celery salt
1 tbs. vinegar
1 cup water
4 tbs. tomato catsup
1½ cups whipped cream
¾ cup milk
Crisp lettuce leaves

Wash and dry tomatoes, cut them in quarters, put them into a saucepan with water and seasonings. Stir over the fire until reduced to a pulp, simmer 5 minutes and rub tomatoes through a sieve, then allow to cool. Beat up cream until thick, add milk and 2½ cups of the tomato purée. Freeze.

Tuna Fish Mousse

1 tbs. gelatine
¼ cup cold water
¾ cup tart mayonnaise
1 cup whipping cream
1½ cups flaked tuna fish
½ cup finely-chopped celery
2 tbs. minced parsley
½ cup chopped fresh cucumber
2 tbs. chopped stuffed olives
½ tsp. salt
½ tsp. paprika

Soak the gelatine in cold water for 5 minutes, dissolve over hot water, and add gradually to the mayonnaise. Whip the cream until thick and fold into the mayonnaise mixture. Add the remaining ingredients and freeze.

Mrs. F. Barnhill, Ohio.

www.ingramcontent.com/pod-product-compliance
Lightning Source LLC
Chambersburg PA
CBHW081627100526
44590CB00021B/3638